NORTH AMERICAN INDIAN WARS

NORTH AMERICAN INDIAN WARS

RICHARD H. DILLON

Facts on File, Inc

460 Park Avenue South
New York, NY 10016
A Bison Book

COLONIALS
1607-1755

While the English and French efforts to acquire territory in eastern North America were marked by continual though isolated clashes, three incidents occurred that can generally be classified as full-scale wars. The first of these was the Pequot War of 1637, in which the much feared Pequot Indians of the Connecticut River Valley were goaded into open warfare with the settlers. King Philip's War (1675–78) was the most costly the continent had yet seen, with Philip attempting to drive the white man into the sea. Philip was killed in 1676 and two years later the war finally wound down, with the white man still in place. The first two-thirds of the eighteenth century were characterized by ongoing warfare between the French allied with Algonquin-speaking Indians against their respective traditional adversaries, the English in uneasy alliance with Iroquoian-speaking Indians. The conflict became known as the French and Indian War, which set the stage for the Indian conflict with the colonists in the upcoming War of Independence.

In 1590 John White painted the Algonquin Indians and their farming towns in Virginia. These pictures, reminiscent of those by Jacques Le Moyne, were charming portraits and landscapes, much subtler—and far less bloody —than the engravings of Theodore De Bry and his son, which showed North America as a land of savages butchering Europeans or each other. John White's Indians grew maize, or Indian corn, in rows and hills fertilized with fish. In their slash-and-burn clearings they also tended pumpkins, sunflowers and tobacco. In lieu of scarecrows, they posted sentinels on platforms, whose cries scared pillaging birds away from the ripe corn.

Virginia

The first permanent Anglo-American settlement was Jamestown, Virginia—it nearly didn't succeed. Within just 12 hours of landing on 26 April 1607, the English were fighting a small skirmish with the native Virginians. But fortunately the engagement did not blaze up into a war. Although there were riffraff among the Virginia colonists, they were less greedy for gold than their Hispanic rivals and more content to stay put and till the fields in hoped-for friendship with their Indian neighbors. It was an uneasy peace; but it was peace. Without it, the tiny English enclave had no chance of surviving.

Perhaps the Indians were curious, or merely patient. In any case, as they watched, the colony dwindled from disease and malnutrition. Of the 900 original settlers of 1607, barely 150 were still alive in 1610.

Above: Jamestown, Virginia, was fortunate in having a leader of the great military experience and soldierly courage of **Captain John Smith**.

Opposite page: Massachussetts towns like **Brookfield** and **Deerfield** often came under siege by hostile Indians who employed fire as one of their major weapons of warfare.

The initial 15 years of relative peace on the James River, which in the long run would guarantee the continued existence of an Anglo-America, was in great part the result of the presence of two towering personalities.

The 'king' of the local Indians was called Powhatan, though his real name was Wa-hun-sen-a-cah or Wahunsonacock, sometimes miscalled 'the mighty Weowance'. (An Indian frequently kept his true name a secret and went by an alias or nickname in order to prevent enemies from seizing a part of his soul by means of this too-intimate knowledge of his name or personality.) Powhatan, who lived at the falls of the James River, now Richmond, inherited a collection of five Algonquin ('Falls of the River') tribes from his father, who had fled Spanish incursions to the south. By the time of Jamestown's founding, King Powhatan had expanded the so-called Powhatan Con-

Above: The story of **Pocahontas**'s rescue of Captain John Smith from execution is believable because of the Indian girl's character.

federation to include 32 tribes and 200 villages, perhaps 10,000 people of seaboard Virginia up to the fall line of the coastal rivers.

Captain John Smith described the Chief when Powhatan was about 50 years old. He was well-proportioned and still able-bodied, indeed strong. But he always wore a sour look. There was a real mix of nobility and savagery in the Chief. Grim and suspicious, he was cruel to prisoners and tolerant of the murders of farmers in their very furrows by his young braves. It took more than a grave and majestic presence for Powhatan to win the respect of the settlers. Perhaps the 19th century historian, Wyndham Peterson, described him correctly as a despot who was cruel, but not pitiless, stern yet affectionate at times, and brave, though also wary and subtle. He taught the English to cultivate corn and tobacco, but sometimes refused them corn in starving times in order to keep them dependent on him.

John Rolfe sent samples of tobacco to London as early as 1613. Four years later, export really began—and the Indians were doomed. Tobacco led to frequent clashes over land, as expansion of plantings demanded new fields, sometimes clearings wrested from their Indian owners. More important, it provided the cash crop needed to make English settlement permanent in the South.

Powhatan left no recorded spoken impression of his opponent. But he must have known Captain John Smith to be a formidable adversary. The Englishman was an ex-professional soldier who had fought against the Turks in Hungary and Transylvania. He had been captured and enslaved by them, so hardships were scarcely anything new to him.

Early on, Smith fell into Powhatan's hands while exploring and mapping the colony. He was about to be put to death by having his head bashed in by a war club when Powhatan's 12-year-old daughter, Pocahontas, intervened to save his life. The incident is possibly apocryphal and has been dismissed as 'an exploded story' by many, but it may very well have happened, so strong is tradition. Apparently, Powhatan's daughter inherited all of her father's best traits without his harsh qualities. Her name was Matoaka, but she did not want it used by strangers. Smith wrote: 'The savages did think that, did we know her real name, we should have the power of casting an evil eye upon her.' So she was called by a delightful—and appropriate—nickname, Pocahontas, meaning Playful or Frisky.

As a child, Pocahontas liked to play with colonists' children, turning cartwheels in the dusty streets of Jamestown. As she grew older, she not only donned buckskins but matured into a remarkably adept 'ambassadress' for her father. Since she frequented Jamestown as much as her own village, she was a pledge of peace. But she also worked successfully to restore captives to one side or another and visited the town on other errands of mercy. After she brought provisions to the hungry Jamestonians, she was virtually adopted by the grateful and hard-pressed settlers. Captain Smith said of her: 'She, under God, was the instrument to preserve this colony from death, famine, and utter confusion.' Later warning Smith of an impending raid, subsequently cancelled by her father, she probably saved Jamestown for a second time, the first being her rescue of the Captain from execution. Smith reminisced: 'Blessed Pocahontas, the great King's daughter of Virginia, oft saved my life.'

Captain Smith knew best how to handle the mercurial Indians and, better than anyone else, he realized the vulnerability of his tiny community. So he was determined to maintain good relations with the Indians. In this, he was backed up by the Virginia Company. Its London directors thought, correctly, that peace in Virginia would be cheaper than war. Smith stood his ground when Powhatan withheld corn, and he was infinitely resourceful in the face of the hunger of his people. To attempt to seal their friendship, Smith crowned Powhatan king in 1609. The old soldier complained that the chief was more interested in his gifts than in the copper crown, with all its significant symbolism, which Smith placed on his graying head.

Unfortunately, Captain John Smith was injured in an accident and went to England in 1609. Red-versus-white relations deteriorated immediately. According to William Strachey, a historian of the Commonwealth, the Indians, possibly stimulated by Spanish embassies from Florida, rose in war and 'did spoile and murther all they encountered'. He reported on a 'weroancqua', or queen, of the Powhatan Confederacy who treacherously murdered 14 men in the winter of 1610. Retaliation was automatic and swift; in revenge, the English burned her village and killed her and some of her warriors in a pursuit through the woods.

In an attack on 30 colonists, only Henry Spelman was spared because Pocahontas, in a re-enactment of the Captain Smith episode, intervened to save his life. He lived for years among the Potomac Indians and was later a skilful interpreter for the colonists.

Pocahontas withdrew and did not willingly visit Jamestown after Smith left. She married a warrior named Kocoum, who simply vanished from history, and she lived in a remote Potomac village. Captain Sir Samuel Argall bullied a chief into reluctantly revealing her retreat and Argall seized her for the Governor. He bore her off into what was euphemized as 'honored captivity' in March or April of 1613. She was placed in the care of Sir Thomas Dale and a Reverend Whitaker.

At first, Pocahontas was, naturally, 'exceedingly pensive and discontented' in her captivity, honored or not. But the patient courtesy of the two men won their ward over. She became a Christian and took the name Rebecca. Governor Dale used her as a hostage to keep Powhatan at bay and to ease haggling negotiations over English prisoners. In seizing Pocahontas, Dale was only imitating his predecessor as Governor, Sir Thomas Gates, who tricked, trapped and killed Indians as part of his 'diplomacy' with the red nations.

Curiously, the kidnapping of Pocahontas guaranteed Jamestown's survival, but not in the way Dale expected. The girl had grown up to be a beautiful woman, and the First Secretary and Recorder-General of Virginia, John Rolfe, fell in love with her. There were those who claimed that Rolfe married her 'for the good of the plantation', but it seems to have been a real love match. Rolfe's contemporaries agreed in describing him as 'a gentleman of approved behavior and honest carriage'. The lovers won permission to marry, both from the Governor and King Powhatan. They were married in April 1614 and peace between colonists and Indians was ensured as long as Powhatan should live.

The Rolfes were invited to England as guests of the Virginia Company, and they took Pocahontas's brother along. Lady Rebecca charmed everyone. She was treated like a princess in London and received by the King and Queen. Starting back to Virginia in 1617, she became ill, probably with smallpox, and died at Gravesend on the Thames below London.

Pocahontas became a legend in her own short life span of 21 years. Ben Jonson put her into one of his plays. A small street or courtyard was named for her in London's Ludgate Hill—*Belle Sauvage* Yard, that is to say, the Courtyard of the Beautiful Savage. The Rolfes' lodgings, the Belle Sauvage Inn, were there.

Alas, history has been hard on Pocahontas's memorials. Buried in the chancel of the church at Gravesend, her exact gravesite is unknown and thus not marked, though a fine statue has been erected to her in the churchyard. Even Belle Sauvage Yard is gone, now, obliterated by Luftwaffe bombs in World War II and never rebuilt.

Peaceful coexistence, tested first by Smith's withdrawal from Jamestown and tried further by Pocahontas's departure, ended with Powhatan's death in 1618. If the Chief had been 'sour', his brother and successor, Opechancanough, was bitter with hatred. No one knows the reason for his rancor, unless it was the incident in which Captain Smith had to poke a horse pistol into his ribs, briefly taking him hostage, in order to get himself out of a tight situation.

Opechancanough bided his time, then chose Good Friday, 22 March 1622, to turn on the Englishmen. He had a good excuse, the illegal execution of an Indian, Nemattanow, for the suspected 'murther' of a gentleman named Morgan, who disappeared on a trading trip to the interior. Murderer or an innocent, the Indian made the mistake of wearing the missing man's hat. Morgan's servants shot him.

In a bloody surprise attack, the Indians killed 347 men, women and children, including their devoted teacher and

Above: **Pocahontas or Matoaka,** daughter of Chief Wahunsonacock, usually called Powhatan (the name of his tribe), was captured by Virginians in 1613. She became a Christian convert, taking the name Rebecca, and married John Rolfe in 1614. Pocahontas died at Gravesend on a visit to England (1617), leaving one child, Thomas Rolfe.

would-be Christianizer, George Thorpe. The toll, about one-third of the colony's strength, was far higher than it should have been. Only a fortnight before striking, the Chief had boasted of his upcoming revenge on the English— and to no one else but Governor Francis Wyatt. Only six of 80 plantations were spared, but Jamestown managed a desperate survival because of the warning of a Christian Indian boy, Chanco. He was ordered to kill his master, Mr Pace, but would not do so and, instead, alerted him to the plot.

Inside Jamestown's flimsy walls, the kin of victims dreamed of revenge for the massacre. Pretending to be timid and fearful, the whites seemingly sued for peace. They invited the Indians to a council to draw up a treaty, assuring them—perhaps swearing on their Bibles—that their lives were sacred around the council fires.

The hate-filled Opechancanough was not to be trusted, either, but if he intended treachery, he was forestalled. The white peace-makers pounced on their red brethren, killing many of them. Unluckily for the plotters, one of those who got away was the Chief. When London chided Wyatt for also attempting to poison Opechancanough, Sir Francis retorted: 'We hold nothing unjust that may tend to their ruin'.

Beleaguered little Jamestown decided that its only hope lay in the extermination of the Indians ringing the settlement. Rather than trust them again in peace said Governor Wyatt, 'It is infinitely better to have no heathen among us.' After Opechancanough's betrayal, patrols were sent to destroy Indian villages and crops, to force the redmen to

Above: In crude woodcuts, early American artists depicted Indian attacks on Colonials, a common – but very frightening – frontier event.

withdraw further inland. More natives were killed in Virginia in 1622 than in the prior 15 years.

Hardly a young man when he fled, Opechancanough had to wait for his revenge till long after an uneasy truce began, around 1634, mainly from exhaustion on both sides. He was reputedly 100 years old or more, and had to be carried in a litter when he struck again more than 20 years after his first campaign. He had planned well, mounting a concerted attack by all of the allied tribes within 500 miles of Jamestown.

Opechancanough's first blow was devastating. On 18 April 1644, some 400–500 whites were killed, mostly on the York and Pamunkey Rivers where the old chief was in personal command. But while he had been mustering his strength over two decades, the Virginia population had climbed to 8000 souls. The immediate defeat stung the colony, but was far from crushing it. In fact, the English, under a determined leader, Governor Sir William Berkeley, quickly seized the initiative from the Indians and drove them back into the forest with the fire of their harquebuses, or muskets.

The Chief was defeated, captured and borne to Jamestown. He lay on his litter, still as the death which he anticipated. His eyes were closed and some said that the ancient one no longer had the strength to open his eyelids.

Suddenly, a guard, probably a militiaman who had lost a relative to Indian war clubs, turned his weapon and fired, point blank, at Opechancanough. The ball did not kill the old Indian but, instead, seemed to arouse him. Somehow, he pulled himself to his feet and ordered his startled guards to send for Berkeley. When the Governor arrived, it was to receive a scolding: 'If it had been my fortune to take Sir William Berkeley prisoner, I would not have meanly exposed him as a show to my people.' Dignity replaced the Chief's burning hatred at the end, and he lay quietly down and expired.

All Indian hope of extinguishing Jamestown died with Opechancanough. But guerrilla warfare continued. The General Assembly passed an act for 'perpetuall warre' with the Indians. This was replaced, however, with a peace treaty in 1646 with the new chief, Necotowance. He agreed to pay tribute to the Governor to acknowledge his submission to the Crown.

The British, in turn, established legal boundaries for Indian as well as white lands. However, especially after Berkeley, loyal to Charles I, was forced from office, the British reasserted their unrelenting pressure on Indian lands, expanding their fields of crops up the rivers from Tidewater past the fall line into the Piedmont. At first they seldom seized fields actually occupied by Indians. But as the population grew, such expropriation became common. Naturally, the Indians resisted and the 'injuries and insolences' they committed, such as trespass on private property or stealing and killing strayed livestock, caused retribution. The causes of conflict were rarely race hatred.

Usually it was the result of minor misunderstandings and simple, but irreconcilable, differences, such as in the understanding of property rights. These quickly ballooned into violence.

Real villainy, masked as Indian diplomacy, again reared its head in March of 1656. The Assembly sent Colonel Edward Hill and 100 men, plus Chief Tottopottomoi and 100 Pamunkey warrior-allies, against some Indians who had re-occupied the area of the falls of the James River claimed by the Britishers. Hill was ordered not to use force to expel the intruders. For no good reason, he killed the five chiefs who came to parley with him. Tottopottomoi was then killed in the fight which followed Hill's treachery. The House of Burgesses and Council alike were aghast at the Colonel's base act. They found him criminally guilty and suspended him from office. The Assembly then repealed a law allowing the shooting of Indians for simple trespass. But these actions did not end the warfare.

When Berkeley was restored as Governor in 1671, he found the Indians to be entirely subjected. Less than 1000 warriors remained in the neighborhood of the settlements of 40,000 Englishmen. The Governor frankly welcomed the local Indians' presence—they formed a buffer between the whites and the 'foreign' (wild) Indians of the woodlands.

In 1675 war flared up again in Virginia and Maryland involving militia and Nanticoke Indians who had seized hogs from a planter for an unpaid debt. A vendetta of retaliatory killings followed. Next the peaceful Susquehannocks were surrounded by Maryland and Virginia militiamen and five chiefs 'protected' by the white diplomatic flag were murdered. The Marylanders blamed the Virginians and vice versa. Both colonies, to their credit, held investigations of the atrocities, but the guilty Maryland officer was let off with the usual slap on the wrist, a fine. Now the Susquehannocks, out of sheer instinct for survival, turned hostile.

Berkeley was considered too cautious in Indian affairs by hotheads who supported his young Indian-hating cousin, Nathaniel Bacon. The latter began to prey on the tribes, mostly on those which were peaceful and friendly. Next, Bacon took on the 'Establishment' itself in what became known as Bacon's Rebellion. He usurped power from his cousin, then chased the loyal Pamunkeys into Great Dragon Swamp and killed and captured many of them. Indians and Englishmen alike were relieved when the despicable Bacon died of 'the bloody flux' on 26 October 1676. His revolt was buried with him.

Massachusetts Bay

Far to the north, the settlers of Plymouth Plantation and the Massachusetts Bay Colony were spared the long years of warfare which plagued Virginia. Although the *Mayflower* had some roughnecks aboard, including America's first murderer, the Pilgrims were better-behaved than most Virginians. Plymouth also had a secret weapon. Disease. The *Mayflower* landed its passengers in 1620 in the middle of an epidemic picked up by the Indians from stray Europeans on the New England coast.

The Reverend Cotton Mather was pleased to see Indian settlements laid waste by sickness. He took this to be an act of God, for 'the woods were almost cleared of those pernicious creatures, to make room for a better growth.'

The Pilgrims found that the ruler of much of New

Above: Indian conflicts meant all-out warfare; women and their children were not safe at all from the scalping knives of hostile redmen.

England was the chief of the Wampanoags. His real name was Ousamequin, or Yellow Feather, but was addressed by his title, Massasoit or Great Chief. He lived in Pokanoket, now Mount Hope, Rhode Island. One settler described him in 1621 as being 'a very lusty man, in his best years, an able body, grave of countenance, and spare in speech.'

The equivalent of John Smith in Plymouth was Captain Myles Standish who, according to an 18th century history writer, Thomas Prince, terrorized all of the tribes around him.

Massasoit may have even met Captain John Smith while the latter was exploring and mapping the New England coast. Certainly, the Chief was a reasonable man; already he had permitted sea captains to collect English castaways he had held prisoner. Even more than Powhatan, Massasoit sensed that peace and accommodation were preferable to war in dealing with the strangers. He became their friend and ally.

On 22 March 1621 Massasoit brought his brother, Quadequina, and two leading chiefs, Samoset and Squanto, to a pow-wow in Plymouth. (Samoset was the chief who startled some settlers by walking out of the woods and greeting them, 'Welcome, Englishmen'. He had picked up a few words in their tongue from fishermen on the coast.) Massasoit may have been reticent, but the long harangues droned on, much of them unintelligible to the English, until the latter, as hosts, sealed the treaty with proper ceremony. They gave the chiefs a gill of whiskey. This caused Massasoit, unaccountably, to break out in a sweat. He was probably allergic to alcohol.

In Massasoit's treaty, land, for the first time, was given away by the Indians, not seized by the whites. The Chief handed it to them because it had been emptied of people by the epidemic. 'Englishmen, take this land, for none is

Below: **Captain Myles Standish**, Plymouth Colony's equivalent of Captain John Smith, saved the settlement several times from the Indians. In 1873 an Armstrong & Company lithograph depicted him as he clambered up from a beach at Plymouth on Cape Cod with an Indian guide.

Above: **Roger Williams,** founder of Rhode Island, was a skilled diplomat. He opposed the seizing of land and, instead, purchased it from Chief Canonicus (above) of the Narragansetts. Because of his genuine friendship, the tribe remained peaceful despite provocation by whites.

Right: The **Pequods or Pequots** of Connecticut, 3000 war-like Indians led by Sassacus, dominated neighboring tribes like the Niantics, but were badly defeated in their 1637 war with New Englanders. Most of the survivors of the conflict were massacred by the Mohawks when they fled into their country to avoid the whites.

Above: **Samoset,** a Wampanoag tribe chief, surprised the Pilgrims by welcoming them to New England in passable English.

left to occupy it. The Great Spirit has swept its people from the face of the earth.' Surprisingly, the treaty worked, though Standish had to punish the Massachussetts Indians —and mount a chief's head on the wall of Plymouth's fort— while Governor William Bradford had to outbluff the Indians when they threatened war.

The Pequot War

The Pequot tribe of the Connecticut River Valley was not a party to the treaty. In 1636 the Pequots became restive. They saw themselves squeezed between the English of Massachusetts and Rhode Island, and the Dutch of New Amsterdam and the Hudson River. In 1636 the first Connecticut colony was founded in Hartford. Trouble was bound to occur.

When the Pequot War began in 1636, it broke out in a strange quarter—at sea. John Gallup of Boston, sailing with some friends, found a neighbor's boat under sail, but in the control of Indians. He fired on the vessel, then boldly rammed her and captured a few piratical Pequots too slow to jump overboard.

Reaction was quick, and deadly. Governor Vane of Massachusetts sent a 90-man force to intimidate the Pequots. The whites by mistake killed every Narragansett Indian they could find on Block Island, then burned their lodges. The force did not lose a man in this swift campaign of vengeance.

Naturally the Pequots struck back, almost blindly, though Roger Williams, founder of Rhode Island, per-

suaded the stronger Narragansett tribe from joining them in an alliance. The Pequots ambushed families in lonely cabins and killed farm boys behind plows. When there was no immediate reprisal for these murders, they were emboldened to put 1000 men on the warpath.

Connecticut appealed to Massachusetts for help. Captain John Mason, an old professional soldier, came to the aid of the so-called Nutmeggers. He was cut from the same cloth as Captain John Smith. Mason was another old professional soldier. He had soldiered in the Low Countries before leading immigrants from Dorchester, Massachusetts to found Windsor, Connecticut. At the moment of the crisis, he was in the pay of the Dutch; his job, appropriately, was to harass the Pequots.

In May of 1637 Mason led 80 whites and a hundred Mohicans under the *sachem*, or chief, Uncas, to a rendezvous with reinforcements at Saybrook Fort. He then proved his powers of persuasion to be superior to those of Pequot's emissaries by convincing a large number of Narragansetts to join him against their old foes.

The expedition ran down Narragansett Bay in small boats. Although a Sunday (no fighting on the Sabbath) and bad weather delayed them, their attack on the Pequot stronghold was a surprise. Mason studied the stockade of 12-foot posts around an acre of ground holding the tribe's wigwams. This aboriginal fortress stood on a hill above present-day Groton, Connecticut.

Mason knew that his Indian allies were unreliable. Chief Uncas was an opportunist who was as likely as not to switch to a winning side in mid-battle. He also knew that Uncas had lived with the Pequots and worse, that their chief, Sassacus, was Uncas's father-in-law.

But the captain was neither discouraged or surprised

Above: **Massasoit**, supreme chief of the Wampanoag tribe, was friendly to the whites, like Samoset, although his son, King Philip, became the deadliest enemy of the New England colonists. In 1621, Massasoit extended the peace pipe to Governor John Carver of Plymouth. He never broke his word though he was sorely tried by the whites.

by the unreliability of his allies. Nor was he intimidated by the impressive stockade or the reversal of usual roles— whites attacking fortified Indians, instead of vice versa. He was pleased just to find the Pequots still ignorant of his stealthy advance. When a patrol reported that there were two gates in the palings, opposite one another, Mason split his force. He rushed both entrances and crashed through them at dawn. He caught the Pequots entirely unaware, but they did not immediately surrender. The warriors fought bravely—like Romans said Benjamin Trumbull—and Mason had a difficult time until he picked up a firebrand, twirled it around his head to fan the flames, and threw it into a wigwam. He shouted over the din of battle, 'God is over us! He laughs his enemies to scorn, making them as a fiery oven!' Mason's second-in-command, Captain John Underhill, followed his example, pitching a torch into an-other tent. Smoke and flames now confused the defenders, and they broke and ran for the gates. There the soldiers shot them down, and the few who escaped were slaughtered by the Mohicans and Narragansetts who found their courage in time for the kill.

Governor Bradford's report read like an eyewitness account of the bloody battle at Groton. He mixed horror with gratitude at the sight of Indians 'frying in the fire, streams of blood quenching the same, and horrible was the stink and scent thereof; but the victory was a sweet sacrifice, and they [the victors] gave prayer thereof to God.'

Whatever the accurate figure of casualties, 600 or 1000, Mason had scored a smashing victory, losing only two men, plus 20 wounded. Small wonder that Cotton Mather would later write, 'No less than 600 Pequot souls were brought down to hell that day!'

But the Pequot nation was not destroyed. In fact, Mason's victory almost turned into a debacle. On its way back to the boats, the force blundered into a war party, 300 strong. Surprise was with the Indians this time. But Mason extricated his men from a near-trap, got them past the enemy and reached the harbor safely, while fighting a rear-guard action against pursuers.

Shortly, the old soldier was on the march again, hunting down Pequots from Saybrook to New London. Those not killed were enslaved in Massachusetts or Connecticut or sent in chains to Bermuda. A few escaped and found havens in other tribes, but Chief Sassacus made the mistake of choosing the Mohawk tribe as a refuge. The haughty Mohawks cut off his head and sent it to Boston to show that they were not involved in Pequot uprisings.

King Philip's War

The Pequot War was followed by a worse conflict, the

first and only major Indian war in the 17th century. King Philip's War, which began in 1671, decided the fate of New England's Indians.

The Narragansetts, 4000 in all, constituted one-fifth of the Indians in southern New England. White settlements were spreading and threatening to coalesce into a broad unit composed of the 5000 Pilgrims at Plymouth, the 17,000 Puritans of the Massachusetts Bay Colony and Connecticut (10,000), plus the 3000 dissidents of Rhode Island.

The exact cause of the war is unknown. The excuse for the war, as usual, was ridiculous. A suspected murder and the execution of Indian suspects. Probably the violence 'just grew'. It grew out of mounting resentment and resistance by the Indians to white pressure. Though the latter still tended to buy Indian land, not seize it, there were frauds. And the buyers did not understand the Indians' retention of fishing and hunting rights, much like subsoil mineral rights are reserved today in land sales. The English saw the ex-'owners' as trespassers, violators of a legal contract.

There was also Indian annoyance at the growing divisiveness in their villages. Missionaries were converting redmen; settlers were hiring others as laborers; and traders were making the Indians dependent upon them. Most important, the Indians felt hemmed in now, between the English and the Dutch and the implacable Iroquois to the west.

After Massasoit's death, his sons Metacomet and Wamsutta shared power. They seemed to be thoughtful and peaceful Wampanoag *sachems*, and the English named them Philip and Alexander, as symbolic gestures of friendship. Still, troubling rumors of a change of heart in the tribe persisted. So in 1662, Alexander was called to Duxbury.

Alexander handled the questioning by authorities successfully and visited a friend, Josiah Winslow, in Marshfield. Suddenly, the chief came down with a violent fever. He died a few days later, on his way home, and his widow accused the whites of poisoning him. Alexander's brother, now sole chief, made no move for revenge, however. On the contrary, he reaffirmed his father's treaty of peace and friendship.

But peace deteriorated into an armed truce. Rumors of war, probably inspired more by Narragansetts than Wampanoags, echoed through 1667, 1669 and early 1671. Since Philip was the most prominent chief in all New England, he was called to Taunton in 1671. This time, the authorities were more insensitive and peremptory in their demands than ever. They ordered the proud chief to surrender all guns held by his tribe, and they seized his weapons and those carried by his escort.

King Philip was angered by such bullying, but he was not yet ready to resist. He signed the treaty and turned in a few token arms. But most of his braves refused to give up their guns. Philip was recalled, this time to Plymouth, virtually put on trial, and forced to sign a treaty of abject surrender.

This scrap of paper was the last humiliation that Philip could tolerate. He began a plan to push the whites back into the sea. To build a confederation, he sent messengers to tribes asking them to send emissaries to secret war councils. For four years he waited for the proper moment to strike.

On 29 January 1675 an Indian named John Sassamon was found dead under the ice of Assawampsett Pond, 15 miles from Plymouth. He was buried there by Indians, but someone leaked word to the authorities that he had not died of natural causes. The body was exhumed and an investigation suggested that the man had been murdered and thrown into the water.

Sassamon was not just any Indian. He was a convert, raised as a Christian, who not only spoke English well but had studied at Harvard. This civilized or 'white' Indian had astounded both the Indian and white communities when he had reverted to what the settlers called savagery, becoming an aide to Philip, then recanting again and returning to the church, where he became a preacher. Then a new rumor surfaced; just before his death, he had warned the colonists of King Philip's plot. Apparently he had been a spy in the Wampanoags' ranks! The settlers, foolishly lulled by long years of peace—and Sassamon's reputation for cunning as well as plausibility—did not believe him. Philip certainly heard of his spying. And Sassamon was murdered.

An Indian witness came forward and named three Wampanoags as the culprits. None of them admitted his guilt, yet all were tried, convicted and hanged. But Wampapaquan's rope either broke or its hangman's knot slipped. He fell to the ground. Taking this rescue as a good omen, and fully expecting to be spared for turning state's evidence, as it were, he confessed to his part in the crime, blaming the actual killing on his two partners, now deceased. The warrior's reward was to be strung up again.

Philip was angered by the executions and by the betrayal of his machinations. But he was still unready to fight. However, his younger warriors soon forced his hand.

The 'grapevine' warned the village of Swansea of an attack. It was a likely target since it blocked the way from Mount Hope Neck, Philip's home, to Plymouth. As the alarm spread from semi-deserted Swansea to other villages, Governor John Winslow sent a negotiator to Philip. The Chief's insolence *must* have tipped his hand. 'Your Governor is but a subject of King Charles of England. I shall not treat with a subject. I shall treat of peace only with the King, my brother. When he comes, I am ready.'

The young Wampanoags did not wait for Charles II's arrival. On the very day set aside by the Governor's proclamation for fasting and prayers for peace, 24 June 1675, some braves—probably without King Philip's knowledge—struck Swansea. They killed nine persons, mutilating some of them, and wounded two more as they exacted 'blood revenge' for the wounding of one of their number the day before by a citizen when they sacked part of the town. Before the raiders withdrew, they set fire to some of Swansea's buildings, as its inhabitants fled.

The Indians next attacked Taunton, Dartmouth and Middleborough, as messengers hurried to Boston and Plymouth for help. In Boston, drummers beat a roll on the Common for just three hours in order to enlist 110 volunteers. Captain Samuel Mosely marched out and reached the charred ruins on the 26th. He took a chance and sent a detachment toward Mount Hope. The patrol was intercepted, but the skirmish was broken off by Philip after he lost two warriors. Mosley lost one of his dozen men in the patrol.

In the morning, Mosley found himself trapped in blackened Swansea. When the Wampanoags dared him to come out and fight, he immediately obliged. His charge demoralized them and they fled. He then marched to Philip's deserted village, only to find the heads of eight white men on poles. He buried the grisly trophies, burned the village and returned to his base at Swansea.

PATRIOTS

1755-1815

All textbooks agree on the length of the American Revolution, 1775–1783. Yet the dates are misleading in terms of the 13 Colonies' relations with neighboring Indian nations. The War for Independence—from England—was halted in 1783. But the Colonists' war for freedom from attacks by both French-allied and English-allied Indians actually began with the French and Indian War in 1753 and did not end until 1815, with the close of the War of 1812.

One man clearly had seen that the struggle between France and England for domination of the North American continent would ultimately be decided on the frontier, and that the Indians would play a decisive role. William Johnson, later Sir William, was a Mohawk Valley trader who was so honest in his transactions with the Indians at all times that he was appointed His Majesty's Superintendent of Indian Affairs for the Northern Colonies. Since he was married to a Mohawk woman, the Irishman had been made a blood-brother of that tribe. Even more important, his friendship and fair dealing won the allegiance of the powerful Iroquois tribe, who had made him a chief.

Nevertheless, the balance of power on the Indian borders after the Peace of Aix la Chapelle (1748) tipped in France's favor. It was a paradox, because the British and Colonials in 1745 had seized France's New World 'Gibraltar', Louisbourg on Cape Breton Island. (To the dismay of the so-called provincials, Britain gave it back!) But the much more numerous Anglo-Saxons clung to the Atlantic seaboard, yielding control of the Great Lakes–Ohio–Mississippi interior to a relative handful of French and their numerous Indian allies.

The French and Indian War

The inevitable collision between Anglo-Colonists and French-led Indians came in the wilderness of western Pennsylvania. Virginia's governor, Robert Dinwiddie, backed by orders from the King himself, sent Major George Washington, all of 21 years old, on his first important mission. It was also a delicate mission and a difficult one. But, young as he was, Washington was already 'a person of distinction' in gubernatorial eyes. He was to ask the commander of French forces on the Ohio 'his reasons for invading the British dominions while a solid peace subsisted', and to call upon the French to retire from the territory.

Washington's 'force' consisted of an escort of just four men, plus an interpreter and the 48-year-old scout, Christo-

pher Gist. He rode up the Indian trail leading to the Forks of the Ohio on 15 November 1753. Once there, he studied the natural fort-site at its apex. He was the first Englishman to see the location of future Pittsburgh. From the junction, a Delaware chief guided Washington to Logstown, where he won the tentative support of some Shawnees and Delawares against the French. At Venango, where French Creek entered the Allegheny River, French officers boasted to him of their plan to take possession of the Ohio River Valley, indeed the whole interior from New Orleans to Quebec via the Wabash, Maumee and Ohio Rivers. They boasted of the power of their line of forts—Le Boeuf, Presque Isle, Niagara, Toronto and Frontenac. True, they admitted, they were badly outnumbered by the English and their Colonial kin, but they considered the Anglo-Saxons too dilatory to prevent the French enterprise.

The creeks were swollen by December rains and too deep to ford, but Washington and his escort bridged them by felling trees and pushed on to Fort Le Boeuf, near today's Waterford, Pennsylvania. The Commandant, Legardeur de Saint-Pierre, refused to discuss the French possession of the land claimed by Britain. But he did warn the young Virginian that he would make prisoners of any Englishmen that he caught in France's Ohio Valley.

George Washington went no farther than Fort LeBoeuf, ten miles from Presque Isle (Erie) on French Creek. But he had seen enough. The fort's walls were almost complete; cannon were in place; 50 birchbark canoes and 170 pine *bateaux* were on the shore, ready to descend the Mississippi to link the Ohio with France's 'lower province' of New Orleans.

The return journey was colder and more fatiguing, made on foot because the horses, left at Venango, were still too weak to be ridden. Slogging along Indian trails buried in freezing snow, Washington composed his report to Dinwiddie in his mind. In his impatience—or distraction—he almost forfeited his life. Wrapping himself in Indian blankets and taking only a gun, hatchet, compass and pack, he took Gist on a shortcut through the woods. An Indian, hiding in ambush not 15 paces from him, fired but missed. Washington made him prisoner. Gist recalled later, 'I would have killed him, but Washington forbade it.' The Major freed his captive that night, then pressed on with Gist to kindle a decoy campfire and hurry ahead all night and the next day before finally resting.

With his hatchet, Washington and Gist hacked out a raft of timber to cross the swollen Allegheny River. But ice floes dumped them in the frigid water and drove them ashore on an island where they suffered terribly from the cold until the river froze solid and they could walk to shore. From there they reached the safety of Gist's Settlement and Washington hurried on to report to the Governor on 16 January 1754.

Dinwiddie, alarmed by Washington's report, sent a small party of woodsmen to occupy the Ohio's forks, the junction of the Allegheny and Monongahela Rivers. He then dispatched reinforcements under Washington. But the French had moved more quickly, ousting the small force and establishing Fort Duquesne. Washington had insufficient supplies even for his weak force, and he was not supported by Indian auxiliaries. Still, he picked up a dozen Mingo Indians to support his 40 soldiers before turning on a party of 33 French and Indians, led by Jumonville de Villiers, which was shadowing him. In the fight he killed 10, including the leader, and captured all the others. Thus, the French and Indian War really began on that day, 28 May 1754, though the term is supposedly synonymous for American actions of the Seven Years War.

Lieutenant Colonel Washington withdrew 10 miles to Great Meadows and erected a stockade which he named, with irony, Fort Necessity. Reinforcements arrived, but in such small numbers that he had to face 900 French and Indians, under the Sieur Coulon de Villiers, brother of the man he had defeated, with barely 400 men. The rainstorm of that 3 July put his swivel cannon out of action and Washington decided to accept the Frenchman's offer of surrender with full honors. He led his men, half of them sick or wounded, out of the Ohio Country and back to Virginia.

Britain finally moved to oust France from the West in 1755, sending over General Edward Braddock. Born in 1695, Braddock entered his father's regiment, the crack Coldstream Guards, as an ensign at the age of 15 and spent the next 43 years in that most exclusive unit in the British Army. His experience in many battles won him the reputation of being a stern disciplinarian as well as the master tactician of the service. Promoted to major general in 1754, Braddock was the obvious choice for Commander in Chief of His Majesty's forces in North America.

The short and stout General Braddock was brave and obstinate. He had, alas, as many weaknesses as strengths. Not only was he arrogant and ill tempered—choleric—he was strictly a 'by the book' tactician, unable to adapt tactics to new situations. He also had almost as much contempt for his own provincials from the 13 Colonies as he did for the Canadians and their 'naked' Indians he planned to thrash. He was clearly a potential victim of his own ego and his own overconfidence.

Braddock arrived at Williamsburg in February of 1755 and spent the spring training and drilling his men before formally assuming command, at Wills Creek, on 10 May. His preparations for the conquest of the Ohio Valley were hampered by inadequate funds, transport, provisions and laborers. The support of southern tribes, such as the Chickasaws, was promised him but no auxiliaries showed up, which was perfectly all right with Braddock. He would count on his professionals to throw the French out. His disdain for partisans, or guerrillas, as well as Indians showed in his supercilious dismissal of offers of aid from the frontiersman, Black Jack, and Chief Scarroyeddy. When Benjamin Franklin warned him that the Indians

Above: A strong, square log fort on the Western border, with a troop of mounted men, was an idealized situation of artistic license.

were not to be disregarded as antagonists, the General tut-tutted him: 'These savages may, indeed, be a formidable enemy to your raw American militia, but upon the King's regular and disciplined troops, sir, it is impossible that they should make an impression.'

The General's personal target was Fort Duquesne, now planted where Dinwiddie and Washington had wanted the key English fort. Other commanders would make uncoordinated attacks on Acadia in Canada, Crown Point on Lake Champlain and Fort Niagara on Lake Ontario. Duquesne was garrisoned by only 500–600 regulars and Canadian militia, plus 800 Indians including both Christians and Chippewas (Ojibwas), the latter probably led by the rising young chief, Pontiac. Braddock expected to have little difficulty in overwhelming Fort Duquesne since he had 1400 smart regulars or redcoats, supported by 450 'blues', or provincials, from Virginia, Maryland and the two Carolinas. He considered himself lucky not to have to depend on the colonial soldiers. They looked like a slothful and languid lot of fellows, hardly fit for military service.

General Braddock began his campaign by hacking a road westward from Fort Cumberland with his 300 axmen. It would be the first such route over the Allegheny Mountains and it was the beginning of the National Road, important in American emigration to the near West. The march began on 10 June 1775 and in eight days Braddock disgustedly found himself but 30 miles out of Cumberland. The column was slowed up by its cumbersome wagons and by the growing number of sick soldiers who were straggling at the rear. For all of his disdain for the 'Frenchies' and their red allies, Braddock was no fool. During the entire march he kept flankers out on each side of the long column, which now stretched for four miles along a 'road' no larger than a bridle path. To flush out ambushers, he kept scouts roving ahead of his advance guard. But at Little Meadows in present-day Pennsylvania the General tired of his snail's pace and decided to split his force. He left 1000 men, including the ill, with Colonel Thomas Dunbar and the heavy, slow, wagons. He then hurried forward with his best 1200 soldiers, plus workmen to improve the Indian trails. Still, the passage through the woods was so difficult that it was 7 July before he reached Turtle Creek, about eight miles south of Fort Duquesne.

Careful to avoid an ambuscade, Braddock crossed the Monongahela River at the upper ford and proceeded down the far bank to re-cross to the right bank again at the second, or lower, ford. He then resumed his march along the rough track, hardly a road, which led to rising ground near the fort.

As Braddock twisted in his saddle to view his column, he must have felt great satisfaction. He had confidence in such officers as Lieutenant Colonel Thomas Gage and Lieutenants Horatio Gates and Charles Lee, both of whom would gain fame in the Revolution. Sir John St Clair's artillery, ammunition train and workmen preceded his smart force of redcoats and somewhat shambling militiamen, well guarded by flanking parties. There was no chance for ambush; no way that the force could come to grief. In fact, he knew that more than one of his officers expected to hear Duquesne blown up, or see it put to the torch by its own dispirited defenders.

Lieutenant Colonel George Washington was so ill that he had to travel in a pallet in one of Dunbar's wagons. He had temporarily resigned his commission in order to serve as an unpaid aide-de-camp to Braddock. He now traded the wagon bed for a saddle horse and rode up to join the General and his other aides, William Morris and Robert Orme. As he watched the advance, in precise formation, of the professional soldiers that 9 July 1775, tramping along to the fifers' tune, 'The Grenadiers' March', Washington thought that it was the most splendid sight that he had ever seen.

It was with difficulty that Captain Hyacinth de Beaujeu, second in command to the Sieur de Contrecoeur, on 8 July persuaded 650 hesitant Indians to join his sortie from the fort with 250 French and Canadian-French. (Probably half of the Indians deserted before a shot was fired.) Beaujeu's orders were to intercept Braddock before he could close with the fort.

English scouts brought back the news that the French were in sight, and Gage's light horsemen pulled up. Harry Gordon, Braddock's engineer, saw young Beaujeu clearly. Wearing a bright red gorget at his throat, he was running along the trail ahead. He even waved, derisively, at the British. But the third volley from Gage's advance party dropped him dead in his tracks.

Braddock was puzzled by the ineffectiveness, otherwise, of Gage's fire. The enemy column, now led by a Captain Dumas, split in two and vanished from sight into the dense woods on both sides of the ravine which the trace followed.

From hiding places behind stumps and the boles of trees, the French and Indians began to pour a terrible fire into the scarlet-coated ranks. The English stoutly main-tained their traditional solid red line, a column 2000 yards long, though it was being cut to shreds by the raking fire. Seeing no enemy to aim at, the regulars fired almost blindly in the direction of muzzle flashes and puffs of gunsmoke. But these appeared to come from all points of the compass and the random firing of the redcoats began to hit some of the provincials who had already left the road for better cover. One English officer in the thick of the fight found himself unable to move, wedged in position by falling bodies. And he not once caught sight of a single Indian. The cannon were brought into action, but did little damage to an enemy scattered in the thick forest.

Only the Virginians, led by Captain Thomas Waggener, immediately left the track to fight, Indian fashion, from the woods. They gave as much as they took in musket fire. When Washington offered to take a hillock on the right with his Virginians, again in Indian style, Braddock spurned him and, instead, ordered Lieutenant Colonel Ralph Burton to seize the height with a frontal assault. Once Burton was hit, the charge collapsed.

When a few redcoats yielded to the urgings of their colonial comrades and dared to imitate their backwoods-style fighting, Braddock and his officers drove the 'cowards' back into formation with the flats of their swords, shouting 'Stand and fight!' They ignored the complaints of the rankers—'We would fight if we could see anybody to fight with!'

There was no doubting Braddock's bravery. He tried to rally the advance guard, still (oddly) in column rather than in line-of-battle, but they bolted in a disorderly withdrawal after only 10 minutes of fighting. These bloodied fellows ran into the infantrymen of the main force, who were coming to their aid. Confusion began to turn to panic when a rumor swept the column that the Indians had infiltrated the baggage train to cut off a retreat. Cavalry, infantry and artillerymen all turned and ran, the latter abandoning their cannon. They spread terror among the workmen, who joined the mad dash for the rear.

Four horses were shot out from under Braddock as he tried to restore order. He was wounded in one arm and in the chest. Washington, who had two horses killed under him and his clothing torn by four balls, was not even scratched. Washington more or less took command as Braddock fell from his saddle the last time, coughing bloody froth from his punctured lungs. He tried to salvage an orderly retreat but the withdrawal, by now, was a de-moralized, headlong rout. As the withering fire continued unabated from the trees, Washington could not even rally the men after they put the Monongahela between them and most of the enemy.

Braddock's shattered command did not stop retreating for 50 miles, until the men staggered into Dunbar's camp at Great Meadows. Meanwhile, Washington evacuated Brad-dock from the battlefield by litter, then transferred him to a wagon. Back at Dunbar's camp, four days after he was hit, Braddock died. He was still muttering to his Virginian aide, 'Who would have thought it possible? We shall better know how to deal with them another time'. Sadly, he also died cursing his redcoats and praising the once-despised provincial 'blues.'

Near Great Meadows and Fort Necessity, the site of his earlier defeat, Washington had the General buried with the honors of war and personally read the burial service. But he interred him in an unmarked grave in the middle of the

road named for him. He then had wagons driven back and forth over the grave to obliterate all traces of the burial. He did not want his commander's corpse dug up and mutilated and otherwise desecrated by the Indians. (Braddock's skeleton, with some of his military buttons, was found by a road crew working on Braddock's Road in 1804. It was reinterred under a nearby tree and a plank, reading 'Braddock's Grave' was for years the General's only memorial. In 1913 it was replaced by a proper monument near Farmington, Pennsylvania.)

For three hours, Braddock's men had been easy targets for the hidden snipers. Sixty-three of his 89 officers were either killed or wounded. Of his 1373 men committed, only 459 escaped being killed or wounded. Gage and Gates were wounded, as was Henry Gladwin, who lived to become the heroic defender of Detroit against Pontiac. His conduct was so brave during the disaster that Gage made him a captain in his new 80th Regiment. Later, Gladwin went with a detachment to relieve Fort Niagara, and he commanded the regiment in Gage's absence.

Christopher Gist and his two sons were scouts for Braddock. They got away without injury, as did Daniel Boone, then a 21-year-old civilian teamster and blacksmith. He unharnessed his team and escaped to his father's farm on one of his own horses. The cost to the French and Indians was negligible, barely 60 casualties.

Braddock's defeat was a disaster. It set in motion a domino-like series of setbacks. Dunbar burned his own wagons, destroyed cannon and mortars, ammunition and food, and stampeded back to Cumberland. The grand campaign was abandoned for mere holding actions. A force of 1000 militia and 200 Mohawks sent by Braddock to reinforce William Johnson, who was leading the campaign against Crown Point, ran into an ambuscade and its Mohawk leader, Chief Hendrick, was killed, along with many of his braves and white followers.

Johnson himself, leading 2200 New Englanders against Crown Point, the French stronghold on Lake Champlain's south end, never even got there. But he was, at least, able to hold off the French and Indians who pursued Hendrick's fleeing survivors right up to his hastily thrown-up log barricades. In fact, Johnson and General Phineas Lyman, who took over when the Irishman was wounded, defeated the 700 French regulars of Baron Dieskau, and 600 Indians. Dieskau was wounded, too, captured and stripped. Dragged before Johnson, the Indian agent treated him kindly, though the Mohawks howled for his torture and death in revenge for the loss of Chief Hendrick. When the warriors burst into Johnson's tent to demand that he surrender the prisoner, Dieskau asked his captor what they wanted. 'What did they want? To burn you, by God, to eat you, and to smoke you in their pipes!' But he told the Baron not to fear; the Indians would have to kill him first before they should take a prisoner from him.

Johnson's surprising victory was the only bright spot for England, and it soon faded. He strengthened his post, dubbed Fort William Henry, but with his men mutinous and deserting in the bitter cold of November, he let Lyman preside over a council. The decision was to withdraw. It is

said that his own troopers now jeered him, but Johnson did not mind. The king made him a baronet and Parliament voted him a prize of 5000 pounds sterling.

Fort William Henry was abandoned; the French retained Crown Point, Fort Niagara and Ticonderoga, and menaced Oswego, still being held by Massachusetts Governor Shirley's men. But matters would have been much worse for England after Braddock's debacle were it not for William Johnson and his Indian affairs deputy. George Croghan, Irish-born like his superior, traveled thousands of miles over a period of 16 years to hold powwows, and not only retained the loyalty of most English-allied Indians but persuaded others to defect from France to England. He also helped in the occupation of France's Western forts after 1760.

For the moment, however, the hard work of Johnson and Croghan was offset by the brilliance of France's new commander in the West, the Marquis de Montcalm. Captain John Bradstreet, one of Braddock's subalterns, had built up Oswego, had launched a fleet of 'battoe' (*bateaux*) to control Lake Ontario, and had beat off attacks as he resupplied the post in the spring of 1756. But Montcalm destroyed Oswego in August. Washington noted that this caused a desertion of English-allied Indians back to France's cause. Now Montcalm put France on the offensive all along the frontier. He distributed so many wampum belts of war that he fielded a force of 8000 men.

On his march against a re-garrisoned **Fort William Henry**, Montcalm wiped out several English parties and was aghast when his Indians not only scalped the dead but also cannibalized them. He felt that he could not stop them. He was afraid that if he tried, they might abandon him, or worse, turn on him.

Fort William Henry bravely withstood Montcalm's siege until it was faced with cannon at point-blank range and the Marquis offered the defenders an honorable surrender. He promised to protect them from his Indians. However, no sooner had the provincials left the gate than his Indians pounced on them, stripping off their clothes, then murdering them. Montcalm tried to stop the butchery. He bared his own chest, dramatically, and shouted, 'Kill me, but spare the English!' In their blood lust, the Indians ignored him. One warrior emerged from a room of the fort waving proudly the bloody severed head of a defender. Others fell on the New Hampshire regiment and dragged 80 men away from the French. They killed 50 prisoners and took 200 more as captives to Canada. There, the lucky ones were ransomed by the French. When some semblance of order was restored by his officers, Montcalm burned Fort William Henry and returned to Montreal via Ticonderoga and Crown Point.

In a minor French setback of 1758, a future American Revolutionary general, Captain Israel Putnam, was captured and only narrowly escaped death by torture at the stake. He was a 40-year-old, nearly illiterate fellow from Massachusetts who had won local fame as a youthful hunter, especially after he captured a wolf in its den. After volunteering in Connecticut's army, he joined Major Robert Rogers's force of 500 Rangers, spying on enemy movements around Ticonderoga.

In an unbelieveable act of foolishness for a man of his reputation, Rogers betrayed his position to the enemy by holding a shooting competition with a British officer. Molang, the French partisan, heard the firing and set up an

Opposite page: Young settlers on the Indian frontier had to grow up quickly. Any lone traveler was fair game to redmen on the warpath.

Above: Surprise attacks on isolated cabins or villages were common because of the stealth of the Indians who crept through the grass.

'We accept your present. You may take him home with you.'

After spending some time with Wawatam's family, Henry finally made his way to Montreal and a free life again.

The closer-in forts, Ligonier and Bedford, managed to hold out against Pontiac's Indians, and the Delawares who attacked Fort Pitt had less luck than Senecas and Chippewas. Although Bouquet was absent, the 338-man force was commanded by another tough officer. This was still another Swiss, a soldier of fortune named Captain Simeon Ecuyer. He rejected the surrender demand, then sent gifts to the Indians—a handkerchief and two blankets, all from smallpox patients in the hospital. The Delawares withdrew, and began to die.

Although Detroit was still holding out, so many posts had fallen that Britain decided (at least in the eyes of the Colonists) to capitulate. A Proclamation of 1763 was issued which reiterated Forbes's early policy and formalized it. White settlement west of the Appalachians was prohibited.

A Chippewa chief outside of Detroit got Pontiac to turn Campbell over to him to avenge the killing of a nephew by a patrol. He killed and scalped the Scot and threw his cadaver into the river where it drifted down to the fort. Like the decapitation of the Highlanders, this atrocity only hardened the determination of frontiersmen to rid the West of these 'fiends from Hell.'

It was up to doughty Henry Bouquet finally to turn the tide of Indian victories. He was marching from Carlisle, Pennsylvania to relieve Fort Pitt, which had been warned by Gladwin. He had 460 men, including Royal Americans and a unit of the regiment of Highlanders called the Black Watch. Bouquet was intercepted by a force of Delawares, Shawnees, Hurons and Mingos on 5 August, but repulsed them in what amounted to a draw. They made the mistake of resuming the fight the next day when he was ready for them. Bouquet now showed his newly-acquired prowess at fighting in backwoodsman fashion.

He drew his men up in a circle around his convoy, then fooled the Indians into a rash charge by having a handful of his men feign a panicky retreat. When the Indians rushed into the prepared gap in his line, his main force, in hiding, opened up at close range on them. He lost 50 or 60 men but he killed a similar number of Indians, including two Delaware chiefs, and drove the Indians away. After this battle at **Bushy Run**, he relieved Fort Pitt. The action quickly cooled the Shawnees' and Delawares' ardor for battle and won Bouquet enormous respect from all of the tribes. He later led a mixed force of regulars and provincials in a pacifying sweep to the Muskingum's forks, securing both the surrender of all prisoners in Indian hands and a general peace on the frontier. Made a brigadier in 1765, poor Bouquet died before his time. He succumbed to fever in Pensacola that very year.

Civilians suffered in Pontiac's war along with the fighting men. Probably 2000 whites were killed, and 60 'Paxton Boys' in Lancaster massacred and mutilated 20 peaceful Conestoga Indians, many of them women and children at prayer with their menfolk. The men from Paxton then marched on Philadelphia where even the Quakers took up

Above: **Ben Franklin** is not often associated with the Indians, but he did play a role as peacemaker during Pontiac's war. Villainous vigilantes began killing peaceful Christian Indians in Pennsylvania. He helped persuade the ruffians to disperse in Philadelphia and later printed a pamphlet which was a stinging rebuke of their actions.

Above: **Joseph Brant or Thayendanega,** He Who Places Two Bets, was a Mohawk chief born in 1742 who was also a friend of both Sir William and Guy Johnson. He fought Nicholas Herkimer at Oriskany and led the butchery at the Cherry Valley massacre. He was the bitter enemy of Red Jacket.

arms to defend the hapless 'tame' Indians there. Ben Franklin and a delegation persuaded the Paxton Boys to disperse after they promised them a bounty on Indian scalps. Later, Ben Franklin printed a stinging rebuke to such wicked vigilantism against scapegoats. In a pamphlet he predicted that the blood of the innocent Indians of Lancaster would cry out for vengeance.

By autumn, some tribes were ready to make peace over Pontiac's protests, and even that chief's resistance ended on 30 October when, with a price on his head since July, he asked Gladwin for peace. Although the Indians had won virtually every engagement save Bushy Run, the confederacy was falling apart. It was not in the Indian nature to amalgamate tribes for war for very long. Some war belts were later sent around by Shawnees, Delawares and Senecas, but most tribes came to terms with Bouquet or Johnson. Pontiac sulked beside the Maumee River and, with his tomahawk, hacked a peace belt to pieces.

By November of 1763, most of Pontiac's power was gone, but Gladwin in Detroit kept his men on an alert until 1764. He returned to England and never saw Detroit, or fair Catherine, again. He declined to serve against the Colonists in the American Revolution and he died in 1791.

Pontiac's last obstinate gesture of resistance was to frustrate at least five American commanders in attempts to take over France's last post, Fort Chartres, near St Louis. After two and a half years of efforts, Major Farmer finally came up the Mississippi with a strong force from New Orleans. The commandant, an old comrade of Pontiac's, St Ange de Bellarive, urged his Ottawa friend to recall all wampum belts of war and to bury the hatchet in peace.

Pontiac demanded a pardon in 1765, but finally accepted a peace belt and attended Johnson's July 1766 conference at Fort Ontario. He was murdered, shot in the back in 1769 by a Peoria Indian companion in Cahokia, Illinois. (Some said that an English trader had 'excited' the Peoria to do the evil deed.) Other stories had Pontiac killed in a drunken brawl, or murdered by two Kaskaskias.

Perhaps, because of the attention paid him by Francis Parkman, Pontiac's role in the West has been exaggerated as well as romanticized. Some at Detroit even called him 'a noted coward'. But nevertheless, he stood as the one great symbol for Indian resistance to white encroachments on the frontier between the French and Indian War and the Revolution.

Lord Dunmore's War

Lord Dunmore of Virginia ignored the Proclamation of 1763 and issued land warrants to veterans of the Indian wars to allow them to settle west of the mountains. A conflict called Lord Dunmore's War then bridged the gap between Pontiac's Rebellion and the War of Independence. Shawnees attacked the veterans' settlements and the Governor ordered out 1500 militia. Sir William Johnson died, but his nephew (and son-in-law) continued his wise policies and kept the Iroquois from joining the Shawnees. Chief Cornstalk surprised a Virginia unit at Point Pleasant at the junction of the Ohio and Great Kanawha. The Virginians rallied from a loss of 50 dead and 100 wounded to beat off their attackers. Shortly, Cornstalk made peace with the Governor to end Lord Dunmore's War of 1774.

The American Revolution

Wisely, the Indians tried not to take sides in the American Revolution which broke out in 1775 with the shot heard 'round the world' at Lexington. Even the Continental Congress asserted that it did not want the Indians to take up the hatchet against the King's men in what was essentially a family quarrel. Still, both Ethan Allen and Washington tried to recruit Indian auxiliaries.

As the war dragged on indecisively, the British general, Thomas Gage, finally instructed Guy Johnson and his counterpart in the South to bring the Indians into the war. The Mohawk chief, Thayendanega, or Joseph Brant, was lionized in London, painted by Romney and given a commission in the British Army. He fought alongside the British and brought most, but not all, of the Iroquois into the conflict on King George's side. Soon, the Iroquois were fighting each other, for the Senecas, Cayugas and Canandaiguas of Brant were opposed by Oneidas and Tuscaroras recruited by General Nicholas Herkimer to relieve Fort Stanwyx at the head of the Mohawk River.

The British stopped Herkimer at the **Battle of Oriskany** but the Patriots killed 17 Senecas and 16 other Indians besides some British. Shortly, the Oneidas and Tuscaroras helped Horatio Gates turn back British General John Burgoyne's march down the Hudson. The murder of young Jane McCrae by 'Gentleman Johnny's' Indians during the march angered all Americans, from the lowliest servant to Thomas Jefferson. Writing the Declaration of Independence, he inserted a phrase deploring 'the merciless Indian savages.'

Brant and the hated Tory, Colonel John Butler, led a mixed British and Indian force on hit-and-run raids during 1778 and 1779. Wyoming Valley, Pennsylvania was struck by Butler's Rangers and Indians on 3 July 1778. Most able-bodied men were away in Washington's army, but Zeb Butler, home on furlough, gathered the families together in Forty Fort. Unfortunately, he then led 300 men out against Colonel Butler. Outnumbered four to one, he was overwhelmed by the Indians. The Loyalist leader lost control of his redmen and they killed all of the wounded.

Above: Older men fought in Indian wars. **David Morgan,** brother of General Daniel Morgan, was 70 when he defended his family from raiders.

Above center: **The Battle of Oriskany** (August 1777) was indecisive and General Herkimer died. As a result of this battle, Indians deserted the British forces.

Above: Tories stimulated Pennsylvania Indians to massacre Patriots in 1778. One of the worst-hit areas was the **Wyoming Valley** where the weak militia was swept aside and civilians slaughtered.

Above: A great part of **Daniel Boone's** relatively long life (1734-1820) was taken up with a personal war with the Indians. His daughter was a captive; he had to fight for his son's body at Blue Licks (above); and he was, himself, a prisoner for a time. But he successfully blazed the old Wilderness Road and opened a new West – Kentucky – to settlement before he pushed on to Spanish Missouri in his last years.

Below: **The Battle of Blue Licks,** fought on 19 August 1782, took place on the middle fork of the Licking River. A band of 240 Indians who had just been rebuffed in their siege of Bryan's Station, Kentucky, were attacked by a smaller force – 182 Kentuckians. The Indians mauled the whites badly, killing or wounding 70 of them in a disorderly retreat. But the Indians' victory at Blue Licks proved to be the last gasp in Kentucky; they could never again mount such a thrust in any force. This marked the end of an era.

Sixteen of them were murdered by one woman, a half-breed who went by the name of Queen Esther Montour.

Then it was Cherry Valley's turn, in the upper Susque-hanna Valley on 11 November 1778. About 30 people were massacred, their homes burned, and their cattle driven off by Brant's Mohawks and the Colonel's son, Walter (Hell Hound) Butler, even more cruel than his father.

Perhaps Kentucky suffered the most. Daniel Boone, born a Pennsylvania Quaker, came to epitomize the American frontiersman. A hunter and scout from the day his father, Squire Boone, gave him a rifle when he was 12, he first penetrated Kentucky from the Cumberland Gap in 1769. In 1775 he was employed by a company of land speculators to survey and lay out roads there. Some of his well-armed surveying party were killed in two attacks, but he established Boonesborough as the nucleus of a colony.

Indians hovered around the fort and in July 1776 kid-napped Boone's daughter, Jemima, but he pursued and recaptured her. There were two attempts against Boones-borough in 1777 and in February of the next year, Boone, now a major of Virginia militia, was captured by the Shawnees. He was quite a prize; they would not even sell him to the Governor of Detroit, Colonel Henry Hamilton, called 'The Hair Buyer', because he paid a bounty on Yankee scalps. Instead, they took him to their village at Chillicothe, Ohio where he was adopted by Chief Blackfish to fill the place of a dead warrior-son. Boone zealously played the role of a happy renegade, all the while plotting an escape.

Ironically, Boone got away while on a salt hunting expedition with the Indians. (He had been captured on a salt hunting expedition to Lower Blue Licks for the Ken-tuckians.) At Salt Springs on the Scioto River, he decided that the time was ripe. Some 450 warriors were gathering for an attack on Boonesborough. He escaped on 16 June 1778 and got to the fort where his appearance astonished everyone. He had been given up for dead; his wife had gone to North Carolina. Boone repaired the rickety fort and mounted and drilled 60 men as the Indians postponed their attack to await some Canadian reinforcements.

On 7 September 1778, 444 warriors led by Boone's 'stepfather', Blackfish, with Captain Antoine Dagneaux de Quindre and 11 Canadians, demanded the surrender of Boonesborough with a phrase which must have stuck in the French-Canadians' throats—'in the name of His Britannic Majesty'. Boone stalled by asking for two days to think it over. He collected all cows and horses inside the fort's walls and had the ladies fill every container with drinking water.

Dagneaux de Quindre informed Boone that Colonel Hamilton wanted the Kentuckians taken as prisoners, unharmed. He asked for nine men to come out and parley further. Boone, of course, chose to be one of them—after he first placed sharpshooters on the walls to cover his party. Dagneaux's offer seemed most liberal. The Kentuckians' freedom required only acknowledgment of British author-ity and an oath to King George III.

But now the Indians suggested that two warriors shake hands with each American. They explained that it was an old Indian custom. Eighteen muscular Indians came for-ward to grasp the 'Kaintucks' in supposed friendship. Boone knew they meant to seize his party, so he gave a signal and the Kentuckians sent the Indians sprawling in the dust. The nine then dashed for the gate. They made their escape under murderous fire from the stockade. Indian musketry had little effect on the stout fort. The defenders hoarded their ammunition and made every shot count during nine days of siege. Women loaded rifles, molded bullets, and provided food and water. The Indians set fire to the fort's roof with flaming arrows, but a young man extinguished the blazes with buckets of water, dodging arrows and musket balls all the while.

Next the Canadians showed the Indians how to dig a 'mine', apparently a trench to give them cover, not a tunnel under the fort to blow it up. Boone simply dug a counter-trench, throwing all of his dirt spoil over onto the point of the other excavation. The Indians, unused to manual labor, gave up on 20 September and pulled out. They had lost 37 dead and many more wounded. Boone had four of his men dead and two wounded.

One of the dead men was the victim of a black 'vagabond' who had been taken into the fort by the Kentuckians. He deserted to the enemy with a Kentucky rifle and became their sharpshooter. Daniel Boone bided his time and finally was able to draw a bead on the marksman, though he was 175 yards away in a tree. He let fly and the black fell to the earth. After the Indians retreated, Boone moved forward to examine the body and found that he had put a bullet hole just where he had aimed, in the center of the traitor's forehead.

In 1780 the Virginia Loyalist, Colonel William Byrd, led 800 Indians and some soldiers to smash Martin's and Ruddle's stations. His bloodthirsty Wyandots then promptly murdered the inhabitants, over his protests, and with a barbarity which shocked even the hardened soldier. To his great credit, Byrd gave up his campaign when he found he could not control his Indians; but the Wyandots, before they left, defeated a force led by Captain Estill.

In 1782, 400 Indians and a few whites, led by William Caldwell, Alexander McKee and the despised American renegade, Simon Girty, approached Bryan's Station—40 cabins near Lexington. Only a few hostiles showed themselves at the edge of the clearing opposite the gate, and they made no attempt to hide. Commandant John Craig was sure that it was a ruse. He guessed that he was supposed to make a sortie against them, allowing the main force of Indians to hit his rear wall, unobserved. He was right. Caldwell had concealed his men in the woods in the rear with orders not to show themselves till they heard gunfire from the front of the post.

Craig decided to try a couple of ruses of his own. The fort was short of water and he could not send men to the spring halfway between the fort and the woods. He asked the help of the women and children. He was pretty sure, though not positive, that the enemy would not upset their plan just to seize them. Mrs Jemima S Johnson was the first to volunteer. She took her 10-year-old daughter by the hand and let the party of 12 women and 16 children. (She left behind her four other children, including the baby—Richard Mentor Johnson, the future hero of the Battle of the Thames (1813) against Tecumseh, and later the Vice President of the United States.) With buckets, piggins (dippers) and noggins, the party laughed and chattered its nonchalant way to the spring and back. Just as Craig figured, the lurking Indians made no move. At the last moment, a few youngsters gave way to their tension and fear and sprinted for the gate, spilling precious water. But not a shot was fired at them.

Above: **Daniel Boone**, the buckskinned frontiersman, was never happier than when in the wilds of Kentucky.

Below: In 1775, Boone founded the stockaded settlement of **Boonesborough**, in the heart of Kentucky.

Now Craig planned his second trick. He quietly sent two riders out to gallop to Boone's Station for help. Once they were out of sight, he dispatched a small force, but one making enough noise and confusion for an army, to chase off the demonstrators—and apparently fall into a trap. He posted all the rest of his men and some of the women at loopholes in the back palisade. He gave them strict orders not to fire—to even move a muscle—until they heard his command.

The hullaballoo in front of the fort flushed the Indians from the rear woods. As they ran to scale the stockade, they got the shock of their lives that 16 August 1782. The wall suddenly bristled with blazing rifle barrels.

After the rush was dispersed, firing settled down to a steady pace, all day long. But only a few defenders were struck down by balls passing between the palings of the walls. However, as soon as an Indian left cover he was shot. One or two were picked off in perches in trees. Flaming arrows were launched high in the air, to land almost vertically on roofs. Little boys and big girls were boosted up to put out the fires. Because of the fort's high walls, there was little danger from direct rifle fire, only from dropping arrows. But none was hit.

Eventually, the Indians tired of taking casualties and, after killing stock and burning fields, withdrew before the relief party from Boone's Station arrived.

On the 19th of August, about 240 of the raiders met 182 Kentuckians on the middle fork of the Licking River. A rash attack by the Americans failed miserably. Seventy Kentuckians were killed or wounded in a jumbled retreat. But at least the **Battle of Blue Licks** was the last such thrust by Indians in force. An era was ending.

Britain and her allies of the Indian nations would have liked the extreme western border of the new American states to be the slanting line of the Ohio River. But a half-frontiersman, half-soldier named George Rogers Clark frustrated their hopes. With just 200 men he peeled away from Britain the Far West of that day, the North West Territory (Illinois Country) which Detroit was supposed to protect. Clark seized Kaskaskia, Cahokia and Fort Sackville at Vincennes in the summer of 1778 with no loss. He did so to let Virginia's Governor Patrick Henry beat rivals Connecticut, New York and Massachussetts in a race for this new West which reached all the way to the Mississippi. But Colonel Hamilton and 500 men from Detroit recaptured Vincennes in October.

Clark set out from Kaskaskia on 5 February 1779 to retake Fort Sackville. He led a force of 170-odd Americans and French. (The latter, like the Indians, were now fighting on both sides.) The expeditionaries marched over more than 150 miles of drowned lands, prairies swamped by overflowed rivers. Clark drove his men as if they were amphibians in one of the most daring and fatiguing marches in America's military history. Hamilton, snug in winter quarters, did not dream that anyone could attack him during the wet season.

Officers and men floundered in icy water up to their hips, sometimes to their beards. There were only a few canoes and pirogues reserved for the sick and those who gave out

Left: In the summer of 1776, Indians attacked not only **Boonesborough** but also **Harrod's** and **Logan's Stations.** The hostiles who slipped up on the latter killed three of its 16 men and wounded another (rescued by Colonel Logan) outside the walls of the fort. Logan later stole away at night to get help to relieve the siege.